These stories are dedicated
regularly stand before classes o_ _____ who often
stubbornly refuse to be educated, and who are
prepared to devise all manner of strategies designed to
disrupt the teaching.

The stories are all based on real incidents and real
characters.

It should be borne in mind, however, that the stories
describe life in the classroom at its most challenging.
There will be many teachers who do not recognise
Kevin, Dawn or Brian, or even Harvey St Jean
Sinclair. They should consider themselves fortunate.

Despite the incidents depicted in the stories, I also
acknowledge that I have had many more positive
experiences than negative, and I realise that teaching is
for most teachers a rewarding and fulfilling profession.

My thanks to Ken Dunn who kept me on the right
track with the story lines and the images.

And special thanks for the front cover.

Not The Noblest Profession Of All

By

Graeme Scarratt

Illustrations by Ken Dunn

CONTENTS

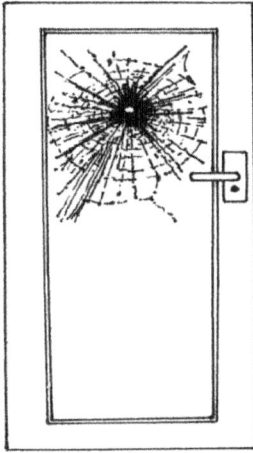

WHEN WILL THEY EVER LEARN?

The bell had hardly stopped ringing, when the first pupil crashed through the door, shattering the glass from top to bottom.

'Oh shit,' said the giant Year 11 pupil, known as Willer to everybody, both in school and on the council housing estate which surrounded it. A veritable monster, 6'3" tall and nearly 16 stone at the age of fifteen, Willer faced no challenge to his authority. He wasn't really bothered by the consequences of his actions, and anyhow, this had been an accident. Besides, who was going to say differently?

Willer's three acolytes were standing transfixed by the sight of the shattered fire door. 'Come on, you three,' their leader shouted, 'I'm gasping for a fag.' Pausing only momentarily as they weighed up the consequences of facing an irate teacher or an irate Willer, they quickly made their decision, and followed the giant out of the school, to seek refuge and their dose of nicotine behind the school's Youth Centre.

Arty Siddle, the Deputy Head was quickly called to the scene. Having checked that there was no danger to any pupil, he stationed two prefects to guard the door. He knew immediately where to go next - the back of the Youth Centre. This was where the villains hung out. As a smoker himself, he was prepared to turn a blind eye to the groups of smokers who congregated at every break to satisfy their nicotine addiction. But damage to school property was something else!

Two minutes was all it took. Approaching the Youth Centre, Arty frowned and shook his head at the sight of the graffiti which covered the walls. Despite the valiant efforts of teachers on duty and the caretakers, the school premises continued to be blighted. Mind you, Arty told himself, there was an old saying in schools that if you wanted to know what was really happening, ask the kids! Anyone familiar with the cast of characters depicted here might be tempted to view the graffiti as a real life 'sitcom' - who was doing what to whom, and so on. And teachers were not excluded!

Arty couldn't help but notice that according to one 'artist', one of his colleagues in the Music department was gay! Surely not, Arty reflected: single, the teacher may be, but he had a reputation as a serial womaniser, with more than a few notches on his baton! Other teachers also featured. *'Mr Bacon is a bastard'* was clearly a popular view, but the teacher in question was aware of the graffiti, and was happy for it to remain for all to see: he saw it as a kind of compliment, an acknowledgement of his high standards of discipline. He was particularly pleased by the respect implied in the use of the title 'Mr'.   Nevertheless, Arty made a mental note to ask the caretakers to remove the offending material.

Willer and his three mates had just lit up when they heard the rasping voice of the Deputy Head. 'Right, you four, put those cigarettes out and get yourselves to my office. Now.'

Despite his reputation as a strict (but fair) disciplinarian, Arty was well liked. To colleagues and students alike, he was one of the 'good guys'; he made time for people, unlike the other two deputies who spent most of their day scrutinising statistics and spread sheets in their quest for their particular Holy Grail, promotion to Head Teacher. Consequently Arty was the Deputy Head that many young teachers turned to, if they were having problems: if pupils were involved, Arty didn't always deal with the miscreants directly, preferring to offer advice and strategies which would be of long term benefit to the colleagues' professional development long after the offending pupils had departed to pastures new, while he himself would be enjoying a retirement devoted to his garden, his grandchildren, dominoes and pints of Guinness in the village pub!

Arty could relate to virtually all of the

thousand pupils in the school, and as well as having the respect of his colleagues, he was held in high regard by parents, most of whom he had taught in his thirty six years at the school. He was aware of his nickname, Arty Squirrel, bestowed by some wit because of his tendency when holding forth about some finer point of the English Literature syllabus, to forage in his trouser pockets for nuts! But woe betide any pupil who used the nickname within his hearing!

Arty was also held in high regard by most of the 'hard lads', boys who proved a handful for many teachers. And it was all down to his passion for rugby. He often regaled his low set English groups with stories of his time with the local rugby team. His battered features and small wiry frame were testimony to twelve years as a dogged, indomitable scrum half. Everybody knew Arty, or knew of him. His was not a face that was easily forgotten! His first meeting with his prospective father-in-law, had prompted the latter to proclaim to his wife and daughter, 'He's a queer little bugger!'

Arty didn't mind the nostalgic digressions which were a feature of his lessons, for with most of his classes, anything was better than Shakespeare and the National Curriculum, both for the classes, and for Arty himself. He had told them how as a young undergraduate who had had too much to drink, he had been left overnight stuffed in a waste paper bin, hanging from a lamp-post. And again, (his own particular favourite which made him both smile and grimace), how he had faced the legendary Test bowler, Frank 'The Typhoon' Tyson in the university cricket nets – without wearing a box! The kids loved it!

What had really made his reputation was an incident during a games lesson. Arty had flattened Willer when he tried to run through him, ball in hand, after the giant had swatted aside all other attempts to tackle him.

When Arty got back to his office, he isolated the four 'suspects' before selecting the twins Eric and Derek Rochester for the initial interrogation.

According to the latest educational jargon, the twins were a perfect illustration of 'cognitive impairment'. Arty despised such euphemisms. He was an advocate of plain speaking; he preferred to call them 'pathetic, harmless little things with only half a brain cell between them, the unfortunate result of what happens when cousins marry!' Arty knew they would tell him exactly what had happened.

'Right you two, let's have it - the truth. Don't waste my time, and don't even think about lying.'

It was Eric who spoke first. 'It was an accident, sir. Honest, sir.'

'Who's responsible?' Arty asked.

'It was an accident, sir. Honest, sir', Eric repeated.

'Who's responsible?' Arty asked again, more firmly this time.

'Please sir, Willer done it', Eric continued.

'You mean Willer did it.'

'Yes sir, me an'im seen 'im'.'

As an English graduate from a prestigious university, Arty had long since despaired at the futility of trying to teach these kids the rudiments of their own language. God only knows how his colleagues in Modern Languages managed, he often asked himself.

The Deputy Head continued his questioning. 'And do you concur with your brother's assessment of the situation?' Arty asked Derek.

'Youwhat sir?'

Arty smiled. 'Is that the truth?'

'Yessir.'

'OK. Off you go. Send in Whitelaw.'

A few moments later, the door opened and Whitelaw entered the room. He was a different kettle of fish: he was a nasty piece of work, and had been from the moment he had entered the school. He was one of the few pupils Arty had little time for. As he stood there, his thin lips wore a permanent sneer, and his eyes stared straight ahead, defiant and challenging. Arty considered how he had never seen the youth display any enthusiasm for anything, nor any of the boisterousness so common among his peers. Why, he wondered, had Willer accepted him into his gang?

'Right, Whitelaw' - Arty in no way felt inclined to address him by his first name - 'What happened?'

'I'm sayin' nowt! I don't grass me mates up!'

'Right, off you go. Send in Willer.'

Willer entered, certainly unafraid, but definitely a little anxious.

'Right, Michael' the Deputy Head began, increasing Willer's anxiety by the use of his first name. 'Listen carefully. I know you did it... but I know it was an accident. So I'm not going to do anything, because the hinge on the fire door wasn't working properly. Have you anything to say?'

'Thanks sir', was all Willer could mumble.

'Off you go then.' As the pupil reached the door, the Deputy Head spoke again. 'By the way Willer, the twins didn't say anything. It was Whitelaw who said you did it.'

When Whitelaw returned to school after two weeks enforced absence, the cuts and bruises were still visible.

KEVIN

In the class of 9E4, Kevin was unique: he liked French. To be more precise, he liked doing the French alphabet, because the teacher always made them practise it by standing up and chanting it in the style of the US marines' marching song.

Kevin also liked guns, and videos in which people got killed. And Kevin was a hard case; he wasn't very big, but he was a tough little so and so, and the class was afraid of Kevin.

Kevin's French teacher, Monsieur S... used this little piece of information quite cleverly because Kevin wouldn't let the rest of the class spoil his French lesson.

9E4 was a notoriously difficult class to teach: classified as SEN (Special Educational Needs, but redesignated by the poor souls who had to 'educate' them as Serious 'Edcases and Nutters), they were every teacher's class from hell. 'Not even Kate Adie would venture into their classroom was the assessment of the staffroom.'

'Sir, can we do the alphabet?'

'Not today, Kevin. We have something else to do.'

Adjectival agreement! Monsieur S... realised that this was not going to go down well. Nevertheless, the departmental scheme of work said he had to teach 'adjectival agreement', and teach it he would!

Monsieur S... began to explain about adjectives and gender, and within minutes he realised he was wasting his time. Pupils were fidgeting and whispering. He persisted.

Before long, he had switched to auto-pilot, and he knew he was droning on. His mind drifted back to twenty odd years ago, to his time in the Grammar School when there was no such thing as The National Curriculum, or even schemes of work, and the notion of teaching language as a means for effective communication had yet to be thought up by someone who had no idea that classes like 9E4 existed.

Without thinking, he asked the question he had come to dread, 'Right; any questions? Yes, Margaret?'

'Please sir, do you play rugby or cricket?'

'Do be quiet, Margaret, and concentrate, or you'll be writing out your corrections ten times each.'

'Please sir, can we do our corrections fifty times each? I like doing corrections.'

And she wasn't joking. Poor Margaret really did like doing corrections: it was her only chance of getting something right! The teacher spotted another pupil with is hand up. 'Yes, Jason?'

'Please sir, what colour is sugar in France?'

'What are you talking about, Jason?'

'Is it blue, sir?'

'What? What are you on about?'

'The French, sir, they're daft: when things go wrong they say 'sucre bleu.'

It's 'sacre bleu', Jason, and it's got nothing to do with sugar.'

The teacher noticed Kevin's hand up. Hoping for an intelligent question, he asked, 'Yes Kevin?'

'Sir, what would you do if a terrorist with a Kalashnikov burst into the room and shouted, "Get on the ground! Now!"?'

'Er, I think I'd get on the ground, Kevin.'

'I wouldn't, sir. I'd jump up, kick him in the balls, and grab the gun, and I'd shout "Now, you get on the ground! Now"!'

Monsieur S… realised that he was not going to get any further with 'adjectival agreement', and he said 'OK, let's do the alphabet, and then you can give out the crayons, Kevin.'

'YEEESSSSSSSS!' cried Kevin.

'Right, you lot, shut up and let sir speak.'

'Ah - Bay - Say - Day - Euh - Eff - J'ai …'

And the class bellowed in unison, 'Ah - Bay - Say - Day - Euh - Eff - J'ai …'

'Ash - Ee - J'y - Kah - El Em En Oh Pay …'

OLD HARRY

Harry Walker was, literally, a legend in his own lunchtime! It was he who ran the school during 'feeding time,' while the Head met his cronies at The Rotary Club, and other members of the Senior Management Team assembled at The Athenaeum for a game of snooker. Mess with Harry, the kids quickly learnt, and you could go hungry!

Harry's smart suit and tie, his polished brogues and his neatly trimmed military moustache made him an incongruous figure amongst the scruffy council estate pupils (scruffy apart from their £100 Nike Air trainers) as they queued noisily for their school pizza and chips. Nevertheless, he was a popular teacher, and a popular colleague.

There wasn't much that Harry didn't know about Tonberry School: this had been the only school he had taught in since qualifying thirty nine years ago. He would soon be saying goodbye to all this. 'What will I miss?' he often mused. 'Sod all!' he concluded, 'apart from the school ginger pudding and custard, maybe.' He had outlasted dozens of school cooks, but the quality of his favourite pudding remained undiminished. 'Heinz puddings can't hold a light', he often told the cook, ensuring he received an extra-large helping!

Often at times like these, Harry had wondered, had been bitter even, that he had never made headmaster, or at least deputy head. His talents may not have been recognised by his superiors in the form of promotion , but his 'old fashioned standards' and his willingness to offer advice earned him the respect of the 'foot soldiers,' as he succeeded in ensuring a semblance of order, at least in his area of responsibility. It sometimes rankled with him that he had heard a whisper some years ago, that promotion had been blocked by The Chairman of the Education Committee, Roy Haller, or Daft Roy as he had been known in his secondary modern schooldays. Thanks to his native cunning and some selective back stabbing, Daft Roy had risen to prominence in the local council. Harry had no time for local politicians, and this one in particular, who clearly resented being labelled an 11+ failure. 'What did he know about life in the classroom?' Harry often reflected.

Harry himself had immediately been aware of what was needed for a teacher to survive in the classroom, and he was comfortable with his reputation as a hard man; and anyway, what was wrong with throwing a bit of chalk? Or a blackboard rubber, for that matter? Harry had abandoned this practice some years ago; he saw no point when wooden blackboard rubbers had been replaced by light polystyrene foam ones. Daft Roy had thought Harry's classroom manner belligerent and unseemly, and not at all appropriate for a deputy head in the newly introduced comprehensive schools.

Harry's experience and seniority were, of course, now recognised by everybody, and acknowledged by his official title 'Head of Upper School': his job was to deal with the troops, the troublemakers, the awkward parents. And by and large, the job now suited him perfectly: not for him the rarefied atmosphere of The Senior Management Team - the theory, the statistics, the new initiatives, the planning, the high blood pressure and the early retirement! And not for him the sanctuary of a smart modern office like that of the Head, relocated in a quiet corridor away from the hurly burly of school life, and from which he 'managed' a depersonalised world where individuals counted for nothing. For the Head, contact with the hoi polloi was to be avoided if at all possible, and when moving between sites, he would always travel the three hundred yards by car. God forbid that he should encounter any of his charges, especially if they were up to no good. And of course, he always made a point to note the mileage for his expenses claim.

There was not much that Harry didn't know

about teaching - if entertaining fifteen hundred idle, unmotivated and largely unwashed adolescents could be described as teaching! None of this trendy Positive Teaching or Assertive Discipline for Harry! Any trouble Harry might encounter was met with a torrent of largely politically incorrect abuse; and so what, if, in the process, Harry inadvertently showered his victim in spit? Or, failing that, he would administer the long since illegal clip round the ear, or the lifting of the victim by his sideburns (Harry had learnt that one from an old colleague who had taught during the 'Teddy Boy' era). Harry knew he shouldn't; he was on tricky ground these days, now that everyone knew their rights, as a result of which, litigation was everywhere. But he also knew that he had the support of most of the parents: many of the fathers bought him a pint in The Woodchopper on a Friday night.

Harry often thought of the 'good old days' when he had come into teaching. 'These kids don't know they're born,' he'd often tell younger colleagues. He remembered how some poor sod who didn't know his 'times tables' would be caned in the morning, and again in the afternoon when the exercise was repeated, as if over the dinner hour, by some magical osmosis, the kid would be initiated into the mysteries of multiplication.

Or again, the unfortunate soul who had been caned for no other reason than the Head hadn't liked the way he wrote the letter 'f'!

Schools throughout the land spawned memories like these. Everyone remembers their first day at 'big school'; the butterflies, the anxieties about new subjects and new teachers, or getting lost in imposing or labyrinthine buildings, and more particularly fear of older pupils who targeted, inevitably, the brand new uniforms. Although Harry sometimes felt that 'a little bit of fear did the new arrivals no harm', he was often called upon to console distressed little 'ankle biters' as they were known, after their tie had been given an impossible-to-loosen 'swot knot', or worse still, after they had had their head pushed down the toilet! Nowadays, regular visits and induction courses for primary pupils, made the transition to secondary school much less traumatic. 'Not always for the best,' Harry sometimes thought, as for some of the little sods, it was a case of familiarity breeding contempt, and they arrived afraid of nothing and nobody, and prepared from day one, to fight the world!

Conciliatory by nature, rather than confrontational, Harry had nevertheless been prepared to follow the advice given by more experienced colleagues. On his first day as a teacher, Harry had been given one simple piece of advice by the Headmaster, the fearsome Boss Howarth, 'If you have any trouble, Mr Walker (no first name informality in those days), just cane the little buggers!' And Harry had done just that.

When twelve fifth year pupils hadn't done their homework, Harry caned them: he moved back the desks, took off his jacket and ritualistically rolled up his shirt sleeves and belted them! The next week, everybody did their homework.

Harry had quickly entered into the spirit of things: when standing in for an absent P.E. colleague, he had devised his own unique form of punishment which he meted out to anybody who was not wearing the correct kit: he would make the offending pupils stand to attention, their backs to Harry as he prepared to take three penalties at the human skittles.

Harry often wondered what had happened to poor little Terry Collins with his snotty nose and black Woolworth's plimsolls 'the epitome of athletic prowess', he had described him, with a sarcasm that was lost on Terry. Why was it that Harry always managed to find the back of Terry's head with a rasping left footed drive?

And forty years later, the latest generation of council estate pupils knew what was in store for them if they crossed Harry: just as their parents had known years earlier. And in a strange way, the kids liked him and respected him for it. He usually bollocked them with more than a smidgeon of humour and sarcasm. Harry's sarcasm was legendary. The kids loved it when Harry had a go at some poor sod, provided that the poor sod wasn't them. Harry's caustic wit could strip paint at fifty yards. There were not many pupils who got one over on Harry: he knew all the tricks and all the excuses. And what's more, the kids knew he knew. In fact, they sometimes genuinely believed that Harry could read their minds.

Harry was sitting at his desk in his tidy office, a cup of tea and two Bourbon biscuits placed before him. There were some days when Harry didn't bother with the staff room, and today Debbie, the young secretary whom he had taught a few years earlier, had brought him tea and biscuits from the main office. Harry had just bitten into his first Bourbon, when the telephone rang.

'Is that you Mr Walker?' Harry half recognised the voice.

'Yes it is. It's Mrs Harrington, isn't it?'

'Yes, Mr Walker. I wonder if you

could do me a favour, Mr Walker'.

Harry paused and smiled as he remembered Mrs Harrington when she was Sharron Longmore, sixteen years earlier. Harry recalled how he had thought Sharron was so dim and friendless, that even if she found a bloke, she'd have trouble coping with the intricacies of human coupling and reproduction. She had proved him wrong, the proof being Wayne, aged 15, Shane, aged 14, Duane, aged 13, and Brain (spelling was not Sharron's forte; she thought she was calling him Brian), aged 12.

Harry thought of future generations of Harringtons swarming over the school. The government's plan to raise standards was doomed to failure! 'The only way to raise standards round here,' Harry mused, 'is to put bromide in the water on the estate.'

'I've just come into town, Mr Walker, and I've realised that I've left a pan of stew on the cooker. The thing is, our lad has gone seacoaling, and he'll be back at dinner time, and if his dinner is ruined, I'll get a good hiding.' Harry grimaced at this picture of marital bliss.

'What do you want me to do?' Harry asked.

'I was wondering if you would let our Wayne out of school, to go and switch the cooker off.'

'OK Mrs Harrington, leave it with me. I'll see what I can do.'

'Thanks Mr Walker. Bye.'

'Goodbye, Mrs Harrington.'

Harry left the room immediately, and went to the main office to look for Wayne's timetable. 'Maths in Room 12,' he said to himself. He closed the file and made his way down the corridor to the Maths' rooms.

When Harry's face appeared at the door, a pupil noticed and muttered to the class, 'Here's Walker!' The rest of the class came to life, relieved to be spared the tedium of the teacher's explanation of quadratic equations

Harry knocked and entered, and the class came to life, and most pupils got to their feet. This traditional show of respect for teachers was often overlooked by many of his younger colleagues, but Harry insisted on it, as an attempt to prevent standards from slipping any further. When two pupils began to talk, Harry silenced them with his trademark withering look.

Anticipating a good bollocking for someone, the class was disappointed to learn that Harry was looking for Wayne Harrington, only to be told by Mrs Short, the Maths teacher, that Wayne was absent along with Arnie Blackwood, his best friend. Harry knew that he had seen Wayne earlier that morning, and as the Harrington house was only two hundred yards away across the school field and down the labyrinth of alleyways on the sprawling council estate, he guessed that the pair were 'knocking off'.

Harry went straight back to his office, and found the Harrington's phone number on the school data base. He picked up the telephone, and dialled. The phone rang quite a long time. 'They're obviously wondering whether to pick the phone up', Harry decided impatiently.

Eventually, the phone was picked up and a voice said, cautiously, 'Hello'.

'Is that you, Wayne?'

'Yessir', Wayne replied.

'And is Arnie Blackwood with you?'

'Yessir.'

'Right, get yourselves back to school immediately. I want you in my office in five minutes flat.'

'Yessir.'

'And Wayne', Harry went on.

'Yessir?'

'Make sure you switch that pan of stew off.'

'Yessir.'

Harry smiled with satisfaction, picturing Wayne's uncomprehending face, with its outer expression of inner confusion.

NEXT PLEASE!

'Next please.' Monsieur S... stood by the door of the library, expecting the blood to drain from the face of the next poor soul to have to accompany him the twenty five yards down the corridor to the cupboard which passed for an examination room.

Before starting each speaking test, Monsieur S... went through the routine of settling his pupils' nerves, explaining the procedure (yet again), and checking the equipment.

'You're not gonna put it on tape, are you sir?' Brian asked with some alarm.

'I'm afraid so, Brian', and he muttered inwardly, 'but I won't be marking it: that pleasure is for someone else'. He considered for a moment the poor sod who would have to sit through the pantomime which was about to unfold. 'And never will £3.25 have been so painfully earned', he mused.

When everything was checked and ready, Monsieur S... started the test; 'Candidate number 4536, Brian W***e.'

Brian wasn't worried in the least: he'd had his twelve minutes preparation time, and he'd had the use of a dictionary. He was confident it would be 'a piece of cake'.

The first section involved role-play: the teacher began his role: *say hello and ask if they have any biscuits.*

Brian responded, *'Bonjoower. Avoir v. irreg vous any biscuits?'*

Monsieur S... wasn't sure he'd heard correctly; then he realised how Brian had used his dictionary, looking up every single word. He fought the temptation to snigger or to say anything, and continued. Brian was the tenth candidate, and the teacher was starting to suffer from the ordeal.

'Christ, it's the kids who are supposed to suffer', he thought to himself as Brian displayed a linguistic incompetence beyond belief. 'How the hell can anyone assess this, as an attempt to communicate effectively?' he asked himself, as Brian continued undeterred through the next stages.

'Pass; pass; pass.' The teacher sighed, and the thought occurred to him that Magnus Magnusson and Mastermind had a lot to answer for!

The teacher continued, *'Deuxième section; fais-moi ta présentation, Brian.'*

Monsieur S... asked the question again, waited and rephrased it, but try as he might to get Brian to respond, the teacher was fighting a losing battle, a fact confirmed by Brian, as he uttered, 'Oh sir, I can't be arsed!'

'Come on Brian' the teacher urged, ignoring the coarse language, 'just do your best.' Teachers conducting speaking tests were constantly reminded by the Examining Board, that the test was a stressful experience for the candidates, and that any intelligible French would be worthy of reward. He didn't want to be accused of not putting the pupils' needs first, so he added, 'Say anything.'

But after a couple of minutes, Monsieur S... gave up on Brian's presentation. Nevertheless, he was hopeful that the third and final section, *'a general conversation on selected topics'* would allow him to say something that might earn him some marks. 'Surely he should be able to say something here; after all he has done French for five years.'

The teacher began, *'O.K. Brian, comment t'appelles-tu?'*

Brian remained dumb and unable to respond.

'Don't show your frustration', Monsieur S... reminded himself. He repeated the question.

Still no reply!

'Dear God,' he thought, 'surely everybody in the universe who's ever studied French can say his name!'

But not Brian. A change of approach was needed.

*'Tu t'appelles Brian****e, oui?'*

Brian came to life at the sound of his

name. The teacher was sure Brian was going to say something. But then Brian thought better of it; he realised he didn't understand after all. 'Aven't gorra clue what you're on about, me like!'

The teacher was startled by the venom in Brian's reply, but he was on the last stages; just a couple of more questions and he could seek the sanctuary of the staff room. And he was determined to stay calm.

Monsieur S... tried to reassure Brian, before proceeding, *'OK Brian, quel âge as-tu?'* The teacher had emphasized the word *'âge'*.

Brien thought for a few moments, before murmuring hesitantly, *'Oui.'*

Monsieur S… nearly laughed; but rule number one was to try to keep the candidates at ease. Nevertheless, some hidden message indicating the teacher's despair must have escaped, and was picked up by the candidate.

Brian sensed that something was wrong; and he panicked. His face betrayed his confusion and anxiety, and assumed the air of someone who had made a fool of himself, or who had committed some vile, unspeakable act - like farting in church - and he blurted out, *'Non!'*

How Monsieur S... kept his composure, he would never know. He wished that the ordeal was over; but he had to stick to the time schedule and complete the test. *'OK Brian, tes passe-temps; qu'est-ce que tu aimes faire le weekend?'*

Brian smiled; he'd picked up the keyword *'weekend'*. He knew this.

Confidently, he pronounced, *'Je un footy; je un drugs!'* He sat back, pleased with himself.

Monsieur S… grimaced, and thought of Serge, the Frenchman who was his colleague, wondering how he felt, hearing these morons mangle his native language.

A few minutes later, Monsieur S… brought the ordeal to a close, 'End of test.' The teacher sighed with relief.

After checking that everything had recorded satisfactorily - the thought of having to go through this again appalled him - Monsieur S… escorted Brian out of the room.

'Did I do good, sir?' Brian asked hopefully, as they made their way back to the waiting room.

'You were excellent, Brian. You're a born linguist: if I'd closed my eyes, I could have sworn I was in France. Next please!'

KNOW YOUR ENEMY

The bell rang, and twenty six pairs of feet shuffled to indicate their desire to leave, as they did at half past three every day, and especially, every Friday.

The teacher announced sharply, 'Stay where you are', and he moved quickly to the classroom door, in case anyone was tempted to 'do a runner', in their eagerness to get home, and get ready for their Friday night of mayhem around the adjoining housing estate.
'Right, before you go, can I remind you to put your chairs in? Oh yes, one more thing; Jason, Brian and Jamie, you stay where you are, you've got detention.'

'But sir, I 'aven't told my mam; she'll be worried, and she has to go out.'

'I don't think so, Brian; bingo doesn't start till 7 o'clock. And in any case, you all got your detention slips.'

'I didn't, sir, you forgot to give me mine.'

'Nice try, Jason, but I've got the copy here,' the teacher said, waving the piece of paper with relish. 'Right, you lot, off you go.'

Twenty-three unruly youths left the classroom, sniggering and gesturing obscenely at their three classmates, while the teacher watched to ensure that none of the three miscreants tried to sneak out.

Year 9, bottom set, was every

teacher's nightmare, and especially on Friday for the last lesson of the week.

When the class had left, the teacher announced, 'OK you three, listen carefully: if you sit quietly and don't speak, I'll consider letting you out a few minutes early. You can even do your homework to make the time pass more quickly.' He knew it wouldn't get done otherwise, and that there would be further aggravation pursuing the matter the following week.

A succession of Secretaries of State for Education had bemoaned the ill-discipline in many state schools. There was no doubt that it was a blight on teaching and learning, and head teachers, eager to comply with diktats 'from the top' usually tried to impose sanctions on their unruly pupils. Clearly, it was not desirable or possible to reintroduce corporal punishment, and in these days when litigation was everywhere, with lawyers quick to invoke their clients' human rights, there was very little that teachers could do, and as a result, many head teachers paid lip service to the notion of sanctions. In truth, many teachers were left to fend for themselves.

Most teachers employed a whole range of strategies to establish control, and to ensure that the recidivists did not rule the roost, and detention was considered the easiest to enforce. Of course, many teachers resented having to detain pupils, because they too had often had stressful days, and were eager to return home to their own family. The necessary paperwork had to be completed, and often, following up missed detentions could take weeks.

Inevitably, there were shows of bravado from the regular trouble makers, and it was not uncommon for them to announce defiantly to their classmates, 'No way am I staying behind!' Fortunately, colleagues tended to support each other; it was definitely a case of 'us against them!' As result a teacher was more than happy to keep back a pupil while a colleague came to collect him or her, and teachers in charge of sports teams were usually prepared for a pupil to miss a match in order to attend detention.

The original, rather pompous, rationale behind detention was for pupils to learn that there were always consequences to their actions. Many head teachers stipulated that tasks should be educationally based, but at this time of day, very few pupils - or teachers - wanted more education. Consequently, some teachers simply tried to ensure that the experience was not a pleasant one, by devising all manner of tasks to keep the pupils busy. Some with a warped sense of humour were quite inventive, giving the detainees a sheet of graph paper on which they had to insert a cross in every square; or they were told to write out lines left handed (or vice versa for left handed pupils); or to write an essay on weird subjects ('describe the inside of a ping pong ball'). Some teachers were sympathetic, and allowed pupils to listen to music while they worked, whilst others used such requests to prolong the misery, by making them listen to records by Des O'Connor! However, this strategy was usually abandoned, proving excruciating for pupil and teacher alike!

Head teachers and deputy heads also sometimes participated, but their involvement did not always go down well with their teaching colleagues, when pupils were left unattended, or were allowed to play on computers, and even, to make themselves a cup of coffee.

At ten to four, after twenty minutes of relative silence and cooperation, the teacher said, 'Right, Jason, Brian, you can go. You, Jamie, stay where you are.'

'No way, I'm going with them', and he stood up to leave.

'No, you're not Jamie; your detention slip says forty five minutes. You deliberately missed your last detention two weeks ago.'

As Jason and Brian left, Jamie charged the door. But the teacher blocked him. Jamie went crazy; he charged the door again, but was again prevented from leaving by the bulk of the teacher standing in front of the door. He decided to change his tactics; he started screaming at the top of his voice, and on seeing his teacher completely unmoved, decided to rearrange the furniture: he picked up a chair and threw it across the room.

When the teacher smiled, Jamie shrieked at him, his face contorted with rage, 'What you laughin' at, you fucking wanker?' He then pushed a couple of desks over, and threw books and papers at his teacher.

As Jamie continued his rampage, and made as if to climb out of the window, the teacher decided that he had had enough.

Noticing that Brian was still waiting for his friend outside the room, the teacher stuck his head out, saying 'Go and get the Head as quickly as you can.'

Jamie finished his rampage, and sat down on the floor, sobbing and shaking.

A couple of minutes later, the door opened, and the Headmaster walked in. To the teacher who often felt, and looked, knackered last thing on a Friday, the head teacher looked as if he was going out to some expensive dinner-dance. His Boss pinstriped suit was immaculate (the teacher was sure this was the third different suit he had worn this week), complete with the distinctive Mont Blanc pen protruding from the top pocket. A crisp blue shirt with matching blue and white striped golf club tie completed the contrast with the bedraggled classroom teacher.

What the teacher noticed most, however, was the Head's hair, perfectly trimmed and blow-dried, but quite obviously dyed as he sought, no doubt, to convey the impression, not so much of a head teacher of a council estate comprehensive school, as of a young CEO of a vibrant, dynamic, trendy specialist academy.

Not even the teeth had escaped the makeover: crowns and dental whitening added the final touches to his handsome, striking appearance. Curiously, however, the whole effect was marred by a mouth, the edges of which, turned down, suggesting a less than happy individual, or one for whom it was an effort to maintain the carefully cultured image.

Perhaps the head teacher knew it was all a sham: he himself had grown up on a council estate in a rough area of town; he had achieved modest examination success, but he had been lucky, being in the right place at the right time in his climb up the promotional ladder. And despite all the costly cosmetic improvements, he could not completely eradicate a rough northern accent, which he had obviously tried to tone down over the years. His rather false accent merely drew attention to himself, made him slightly ridiculous. He hated those head teachers from more prestigious schools and colleges, who referred to him as 'The Posh Geordie'.

'What's the problem, Mr S...? I've just come from having tea with the Chairman of Governors before the governors' meeting. You sent Brian to tell me that there was a problem, an emergency.'

The teacher looked at his Head, gesturing to the chaos, unable to believe that the head teacher hadn't noticed.

'What's been going on?' the Head asked.

'Jamie here took exception to being kept in detention.' And he added, before the Head asked, 'He's had all the proper notice, and a verbal reminder in the last lesson. Oh yes; and he called me a fucking wanker.'

The head teacher grimaced at the obscenities. Childless, and the owner of a huge detached house some thirty miles away literally, and a thousand miles figuratively, from the rundown place where he worked, he was no longer comfortable with the crudeness of the language of the streets.

'Is this true, Jamie?'

'Yeah, cos he is.'

The Head stood for a couple of minutes, uncertain how to proceed. This wasn't a situation in which he was comfortable; he usually left such unpleasantness to his deputies, or the pastoral team. He was much more at ease in the company of Education Ministers, MPs and local dignitaries, and above all, members of the media. 'You know, Jamie, you used to be such a lovely lad when you were in Year 7.'

He paused. Jamie said nothing.

'Right, Jamie,' the Head continued, 'I'd like you to apologise to Mr S...'

Silence.

'Will you say sorry, Jamie?'

'No.'

'Come on, Jamie; for me.'

'No.'

'Please Jamie.'

'No.'

'Why not, Jamie, it's only a little word.'

'Cos he's a twat.'

The Head pulled a face. 'Look Jamie,' he said, trying to inject some severity into his voice, 'if you don't say sorry, you'll be in trouble.'

'I don't care.'

'I'm warning you, Jamie.'

No response.

Mr S... was starting to become impatient with this lack of action. He was certainly unimpressed by this pathetic attempt at a show of authority. He coughed to show his impatience.

'OK Jamie,' the head teacher said, 'I'm going to count to three, and I want you to say sorry. One.'

No response.

'Two.'

No response.

'I'm warning you, Jamie.'

No response.

'Three.'

Mr S... raised his eyes, pleased that the incident was about to be resolved.

The Head continued; 'Shall I say sorry for you, Jamie? Would you like that?'

'Whatever!'

'OK.' The Head seemed embarrassed to look at Jamie's teacher, adopting a pathetic, meek, sheepish look which seemed to say 'I wouldn't normally deal with the situation like this, but I need to get back to the Chairman of Governors.'

The teacher was appalled!

'Sorry Mr S...'

Mr S... looked stunned. He was seething inwardly; if this was what you needed to become a head teacher, you could forget it!

'OK,' the Head continued, 'that's settled.'

Mr S… gave a shake of the head, not caring if the head teacher saw it as a slight on his authority. He wasn't sure what sort of retribution he had expected, but he was certainly unprepared for what had taken place. And he certainly wasn't prepared for what followed.

After a few moments' silence, the Head had made up his mind. 'Right, come with me' he said, attempting to speak with authority, and then, his voice softening to almost a whisper, he asked, 'Shall we see if there are any cakes left from the governors' tea?'

He put his arm around Jamie's shoulders, and moved towards the door, before turning, and adding, 'I'm sure Mr S… won't mind tidying the room up.'

NEVER A DULL MOMENT!

'Sir, will you tell 'im?'

'Yes Dawn, what is it?'

'It's 'im , sir, it's Steven.'

'Yes Dawn, I know who he is; I've been his Form Teacher for nearly four years.'

'Yes sir, but will you tell 'im?'

'Yes Dawn, tell him what?'

'Sir, he called me a stupid, fat cow.'

'Certainly, Dawn, which bit are you objecting to?'

'Eh?' Dawn muttered, before exclaiming, 'All of it!'

'In you go, Dawn'.

Dawn tutted, and stomped into the classroom; 'God, I 'ate 'im!' she said, before adding, 'And my mother hated 'im as well.'

And so began the weekly pantomime that was the PHSE lesson.

Dawn knew she was a figure of fun, but still she persisted in winding people up. Her teacher accepted, and tolerated this display of squabbling and name calling as part of the adolescent mating rituals which existed, he imagined, in every school in the land. Others saw this as a form of bullying, and would no doubt have viewed his response as reprehensible.

Nevertheless, the teacher often wondered why Dawn insisted in drawing attention to herself, as she was not what might be called one of life's beautiful people; lack of self-esteem, the educational psychologists would say. And she always rose to the bait: when someone shouted, 'Sir, Steven fancies Dawn,' Dawn gave a little smirk to herself, until someone else announced,

'He should have gone to Specsavers!'

With the class in fits of laughter, Dawn replied as she usually did, by leaping out of her seat, and slapping the culprit across the head. 'Shut yer fat gob, you.'

Steven was no oil painting either, for that matter. But the teacher had a bit of a soft spot for both Steven and Dawn.

As far as Steven was concerned, a genial oaf was as good a description as any, for despite his regular squabbles with Dawn, he wasn't really malicious; he simply had a habit of speaking without engaging his brain. Steven and his teacher shared a passion for rugby, and Steven was the star of the Under-15 team, coached by his form teacher. And when the teacher had revealed that he had grown up near to where Steven lived, the class had been incredulous, with someone shouting out, 'But sir, they're all smack 'eads there.'

Dawn also had her moments when she was both likeable and pleasant; she was the first to sympathise when the real trouble makers threatened to make the teacher's life unbearable. She also laughed at his jokes, could take a joke, and could usually accept her teacher's criticism without rancour.

Reports from the nursery where she had been placed on work experience, spoke of her caring manner when dealing with babies and toddlers, which was probably just as well, since, if the tittle tattle of the classroom was to believed, it wouldn't be long before she was having kids of her own, unless the PHSE lessons in contraception and family planning gave her food for thought.

All in all, her teacher concluded, Dawn was a kid with a good heart, in spite of the dire circumstances of her home life.

'Who knows,' he mused, 'she and Steven could do worse than have each other as a partner', though he wasn't sure he would want to teach any of their offspring.

The teacher knew that an important part of his role was to counter the powerful influences which emanated from their homes. He tried to relate to them by talking about his own upbringing; surely they couldn't fail to be impressed that the four sons of his bus-driver father, had all gone to university. They were not impressed in the slightest: he usually found himself the object of ridicule or sarcastic comments! When he told them how he had been caned at school - an 'all boys' school' - for not wearing his cap, the comments came thick and fast.

'An 'all boys' school'!'

'A cap!'

'Were you all gay, sir?'

Most pupils saw no point in education; they were all convinced they were going to be rich and famous, courtesy of the Premier League or X-Factor. They were certainly not impressed by his career path; five years at university, to become a teacher. Big deal!

The more boring subjects – credit cards, mortgages, income tax, immigration – were given equally short shrift! How many times had he been asked by members of his class, 'Sir, do you think it's right that all these foreigners should come over here, and nick our jobs?'

'I don't think foreigners do take all our jobs', the teacher replied, hoping that this might lead to a sensible discussion.

'Me dad says they do. And me granddad says the same.'

'What does your dad do?'

'He's on the dole, sir.'

'And what about your granddad?'

'He 'asn't got no job neither.'

'Yes, but I'm sure they want you to do well at school.'

'They both say I don't need no

education, and I'll be alright provided I do three things.'

'And what three things are they?' the teacher asked, wondering what gems of wisdom were coming next.

'Don't get married, don't get a job and don't buy a house.'

'Too right' said his neighbour, and they exchanged 'high fives'.

The teacher soon lost interest in this argument which he knew he couldn't win, as the 'discussion' quickly degenerated into name calling etc.

In view of the regular chaos and mayhem, the teacher often wondered what exactly was the raison d'être of PHSE.

In all his years of teaching in this deprived unemployment blackspot, he had never encountered a more bigoted cross section of society, which was not surprising as he had taught their parents, and in some cases, grandparents. He could never understand how the town had elected socialist MPs for generations; self-interest, based on benefits and handouts, he assumed.

He nevertheless felt a little hypocritical when he wrote in pupils' leaving books, 'Be happy', or 'Dare to dream'; definitely 'puke inducing', but the kids liked it, and he didn't have the heart to write 'Welcome to the real world', or 'God help you if you're ever lucky enough to get a job!'

PHSE - Personal, Health and Social Education - where had that come from? A question he and many of the more traditionalist teachers had asked themselves many times. He had trained to be a teacher, and expected to teach his subject, maybe act as a form teacher, taking the register and collecting dinner money, and checking absence notes.

But now, the school seemed obsessed with the 'pastoral system': now he was expected to be a councillor, a surrogate father, and worst of all, a buddy! Even in the classroom when a lesson was being taught, there seemed to be more 'minders' than pupils, with classroom assistants allocated to any pupil considered a potential troublemaker, or in need of help with reading or writing etc.

In order to prepare teachers to teach PHSE, there had, of course, been a couple of days of in-service training, designed to raise their awareness of all manner of things which the form teacher was expected to embrace before he could truly 'understand' his charges – dyslexia, dyspraxia, ADHD, Asperger Syndrome… The list was endless. And what exactly did PHSE lessons achieve? He knew the theory of course; it had been introduced into the curriculum to provide pupils with many of the lessons for life that they no longer received at home: respect for others, social graces, and an understanding of the world in which they would soon find themselves - cast adrift, he imagined all too clearly.

The intention was that teaching would not be didactic. Instead, pupils would be allowed the opportunity to take the lead, to shape the discussions, to express themselves.

There had been none of this nonsense in his schooldays, or even when he had begun his teaching career. Pupils from an assortment of backgrounds had mixed freely, and had got on well with everybody else. He admitted that there had been altercations and the odd punch-up, but they had not needed to be taught social graces. His teachers had been able to eat their lunch in polite conversation with their pupils. Now he was expected to keep the peace, as fights threatened to break out over accusations of theft, 'Sir, he's just nicked one of me roasties!'

Of course, many of the topics to be discussed were controversial in the eyes of many people, both inside and outside education. Some teachers felt uncomfortable, unqualified and ill equipped to 'discuss' subjects such as drug addiction, child abuse, sexually transmitted diseases, unwanted pregnancies, and so on.

Not that the pupils minded; they revelled in the discomfort of their teachers when during a discussion on contraception and family planning, the teachers were expected to take the lead, by putting a condom on a banana!

'Sir, does your wife work at the Johnny Club?' was a question he was often asked, even though everyone knew the answer,

'Er, yes, she is part of a team which gives contraception advice to young people.' And he knew what would follow.

'Any freebies, sir?' This always produced guffaws!

Whether they were simply taking advantage of the informal style of the lessons, or whether they really did despise the morals and standards of the older generation, he couldn't be sure, but some pupils saw the topics under discussion as the ideal opportunity to put the teachers on the spot, by asking personal questions designed to embarrass and to cause mayhem. Sex, with all the attendant issues, was the topic most teachers dreaded.

'Sir, do you know what a 69 is?'

The class went quiet.

'Of course, Dawn. Doesn't

everybody?'

Sniggers.

'What is it then, sir? Tell us.'

More sniggers, and the class waited in anticipation.

'It's the same as a 99, but without the chocolate flake!'

'Aw, sir…'

'Right. Let's change the subject.'

In his role as mentor to newly qualified teachers, he always stressed the need for a sense of humour, and an ability to think on your feet. It had certainly helped him cope with potentially difficult situations.

The teacher was dismayed that kids today seemed to have no sense of responsibility, no sense of community spirit, no sense even, of camaraderie. It used to be the case that kids refused to tell tales on their friends; now they took delight in causing trouble for their mates – and their teachers of course – for no other reason that it was 'a laugh'! They had never known corporal punishment, and any time a teacher had to spend remonstrating with a pupil, or filling out the interminable forms, meant less time the teacher had to teach them, and less time they were required to think.

He expected, as part of his teaching duties, to have to deal with stroppy adolescents. His head teacher, however, always tried to make him feel guilty of being unnecessarily strict whenever an altercation arose, and he tried to impose his standards on his classes. 'Of course, part of our job is to help these young people through this difficult phase in their lives.'

'Yeah, but you should try a stint in the classroom, mate, trying to engage their interest in such mysteries as simultaneous equations, the principle of moments, or the French imperfect tense,' he felt like replying.

Part of the rationale of PHSE was that the lessons were to facilitate closer contacts between school and family. The teacher was certainly expected to have more contact with parents than when he had been a mere teacher of his subject, and there were indeed benefits to these closer ties. Over a pupil's five years in secondary school, he had got to know the parents of most pupils, and they were often on first name terms. As a result, family concerns and problems could be treated sensitively; it was not unknown for some salacious marital details to emerge!

On the other hand, some parents felt entitled to talk to him like a three years old child.

Teachers of an earlier age could not have imagined some of the duties he was expected to carry out as a form tutor. He was expected to check that pupils were not chewing, and not wearing lipstick, jewellery, nail varnish and so on. They would not believe that, as per the instructions of his Head of Year, he was expected to keep in his desk nail varnish remover! He was also expected to check that the school uniform was 'worn correctly': ties had to be fastened properly, shirts had to be tucked in, and skirts must not be too revealing!

On which subject, he was occasionally called upon to pacify an irate mother who accused him of 'picking on our Mandy', because he made her remove her jewellery and make up, and wear her skirt more modestly.

The teacher tried to turn the tables on the doting mother by suggesting that on the contrary, Mandy picked on him by arriving at school every morning and every afternoon 'wearing full make up, and dressed as if she was ready for a night on the town.'

The mother was having none of it, because she 'knew for a fact that all the girls came dressed like that.' And she had warned him that he 'had better look after her daughter's confiscated jewellery, because it cost her six hundred quid!'

PHSE was probably the most unpopular lesson among teachers and pupils alike. It was known as the 'draw a poster lesson!' - about anti-drugs, anti-smoking, anti-alcohol, anti-vandalism, anti-litter, and so it went on. He supposed that in itself, this served a purpose of sorts; at least it kept them occupied. Inevitably, however, it led to squabbles; about pens ('Sir, will you tell Steven to lend me the red?'), about glue ('Sir, will you tell Steven to stop wiping the glue on me?'), about scissors ('Sir, will you tell Steven to stop stabbing me?'). The squabbles and the disruption were endless.

His heart always sank whenever he read the instructions in the lesson notes '*Ask the class to work in a group.*' He always noted the word '*Ask*', usually underlined. It was typical of the 'touchy feelies' on the pastoral team who seemed more and more to be influencing the running of the school.

The need for co-operation was one thing, but having to seek the permission of the class, really made his blood boil! And group work, how he hated that: it simply meant that that the kids had four or five extra people to talk to, to kick under the table, to 'wind up.' 'Was there really anything wrong,' he often asked himself, 'with pupils sitting in rows, facing the front?'

There was always somebody in education to come up with new ideas to improve standards. The teacher considered himself reasonably enlightened, and was prepared to give 'the thinkers' the benefit of the doubt. But he sometimes wondered how far from the truth was the philosophy of the old lags in the staffroom. 'If they really want to improve standards, they should send the little buggers down the pits, until they're fourteen. Then let them come to school, and they might appreciate education.'

'Why fix something if it aint broke?' was a view that many teachers held.

In the 'old days' pupils new to secondary school were in 'the first year'. Now they were Year 7. Second year pupils were now Year 8, and so on. He also remembered how some bright, liberal education officer had protested at the discrimination inherent in the labelling of classes as A,B,C,D etc. He had therefore advocated the introduction of random lettering, such as P,Q,R,S.

Unfortunately, this had had repercussions in one school, when following a playground incident, a teacher had requested details of name and form from a fifteen years old boy. The name had been given freely enough, but when asked for his form, the boy had snarled, '4Q, sir.'

The experiment was soon abandoned.

Above all, the teacher was expected to

remain positive. And in truth, some aspects of the course seemed to work; in encouraging the pupils to show respect to others, to accept the right of people to hold a different opinion, he suggested they treat others as they would want to be treated themselves. It seemed to strike a chord. He invited each pupil to say something positive about his neighbour. Despite the embarrassment, this was not the disaster he was expecting. Many pupils were smiling, clearly feeling good about themselves, which was not a regular occurrence.

Then the bell rang, and he dismissed the class, thankful that the weekly ordeal was over and also that the lesson had finished on a positive note. And then, of course, Steven brought him down to earth. As he left, Steven barged past pupils waiting outside for a detention, 'Gerrout me way, you stupid lezzie' he shouted at a girl.

The teacher called Steven back. 'Steven, what have we just been doing, about respect for others?'

'Yeah, sir, but she's not in our class!' and he raced off down the corridor.

UP NORTH

All newly appointed head teachers make promises.

They make promises to their new governors, to their new staff, to new parents, and to new pupils.

They make promises to themselves.
Perhaps they will remodel the school uniform. Perhaps they will focus on, and improve the school's academic record. Perhaps they will oversee a new regime of discipline and respect.

They often sum up their intentions as a desire to recreate the education which they themselves had enjoyed.

Harvey St Jean Sinclair did all of these things. His new staff, disillusioned and weary, had long stopped listening to the inevitable clichés presented to them by the 'men in suits.'

A combination of family connections, old school tie influence and success as head teacher in his previous school, had resulted in Harvey St Jean Sinclair being designated a Super Head, one of the elite of the elite who commanded a high salary to work their magic in often very difficult circumstances.

All Super Heads were expected to believe that they could make a difference wherever they were appointed. Harvey St Jean Sinclair, therefore, viewed his latest challenge with something resembling missionary zeal: he was expected to 'turn around' a comprehensive school in the north-east of England. He would then, he decided, contemplate early retirement back to the Home Counties.

Now the new head teacher was addressing his demoralised troops for the first time. So only a few eyebrows were raised when he announced his intention to reform the staff cricket team. Team spirit, he reasoned, would be engendered through the wonderful game that was cricket, and would be the key to improvements in every aspect of school life.

Before taking up his appointment at the start of the Summer Term, the new head teacher had made a few telephone calls, and had discovered that there was an inter-school competition for staff cricket teams. He had no doubts that this was exactly what the dispirited, demotivated staff needed. The memories came back to him from his own happy time at school; he remembered keenly contested matches between the Staff and the 1st XI, when the timetable was suspended, and the whole school would be taken out to The Lawn.

Harvey St Jean Sinclair learned a few days later, that the Staff XI would be travelling for their first match, to a comprehensive school in H... a neighbouring former mining village, where hatred for Maggie Thatcher was still vitriolic, and still a topic of conversation in many homes, pubs and working men's clubs. Although their neighbours six miles down the coast could hardly be blamed for the actions of the former Prime Minister, the ex-mining village still harboured resentment as the town had benefited from various grants and subsidies, allowing their communities to flourish, whilst theirs had shrunk and withered.

When he sought information and advice from his PE staff, the Head was disappointed that they did not share his enthusiasm. They tried to warn him that you did not go to H... without good cause, and a game of cricket did not, in their eyes, constitute a good cause. Any sporting contact should be avoided at all costs. When he sought clarification as to what they meant, the Head received the reply from the oldest, most cynical member of the department, 'Put it this way...' he snarled in imitation of Long John Silver, '... them's that dies'll be the lucky ones!'

Not fully understanding the significance of the reply, the Head chose to ignore the warnings; he simply reassured himself that his position of authority, and his public school background, had prepared him for anything. Nevertheless, he promised himself that he would again read the biography of Douglas Jardine, to seek inspiration for dealing with unsavoury characters. He himself may not exactly have had 'the common touch', but he convinced himself that good breeding, an expensive education and his received pronunciation would always prevail.

Once the Head had left, the murmurings started: 'He must be mad,' someone said.

'You can count me out,' said another.

When a couple of young NQTs voiced enthusiasm for the idea, the old lags in the staffroom saw fit to enlighten them.

'You're not from round here, are you son?'

'No, but what's that got to do with anything?'

'They're not like us, son, and they don't like us.'

'Surely, it's only a game of cricket.'

'They're inbred yakkers, with high foreheads, and arms which reach down to the ground. And we're the posh townies, at least in their eyes. They relish every opportunity to, how shall I put this, stuff it right up us!'

'But we've got some decent players, I've heard.'

'And so have they. And they're bound to bring in a couple of ringers. You'll find out when you go out to bat, that they have an innate propensity for violence.'

'What do you mean?' asked the novice PE teacher, wishing he hadn't sounded so enthusiastic, and wondering what he had let himself in for.

'Oh you know, the usual... short pitched deliveries... about four an over... plus the odd beamer. Just make sure you wear a helmet... and a chest pad, and two arm pads. Oh and don't forget your box.'

'Too right,' another voice added, 'you're getting married soon, so make sure you look after the family jewels.'

During the next few weeks, the forthcoming cricket match was a frequent topic of conversation in the staffroom. Most of those who had been cajoled or coerced into playing showed little enthusiasm as the day drew near. But the new Head saw himself as being made of sterner stuff: he was sure that his powers of leadership, not to mention his prowess with 'the old willow' would ensure victory.

It was a fine, balmy evening, a sign perhaps that everything would turn out well. Or so the Head hoped.

But as they drew near to the village cricket ground where the school team played its fixtures, it became all too clear that

Harvey St Jean Sinclair was entering a world which was totally alien to him. The flat tracks and manicured lawns of Esher, Cheltenham and the like, were a million metaphorical miles away. A number of youths loitered by the entrance, smoking all manner of dubious substances. The head teacher failed to notice, but Bob the caretaker was all too familiar with the afterschool activities practised at his own school.

'Why aren't they at home doing their homework?' the head teacher asked Bob, who had also been recruited to play. The caretaker wasn't sure if he was expected to reply, so he said nothing. He was more attentive to avoiding the broken glass and dog turds, which littered the outfield. At well over eighteen stone, Bob himself didn't feel threatened, but he was anxious to move the Head on before some comment would oblige him to intervene.

They reached the dressing room without incident, and they waited for the rest of the team to arrive.

Harvey St Jean Sinclair had come already dressed for the game, resplendent in cream flannels, cravat and of course his prized possession, his distinctive MCC cap. If he noticed the assortment of coloured trousers, pullovers and footwear worn by his team, the head teacher made no comment.

Eager to get started, The Head left his team and went to introduce himself to the opposing captain.

'Yareet marrer?' the opposing captain said cheerfully enough, flicking a half smoked hand rolled cigarette deftly into a cardboard box which served as a litter bin. His massive proffered hand with Cumberland pork sausages for fingers enveloped that of Harvey St Jean Sinclair, who tried not to wince, and rescued his hand as quickly as possible. He had a fleeting premonition that this was a sign of things to come. He tried to dismiss it from his mind.

'Howay bonnie lad, let's get this show on the road,' announced the H... captain, adding as he noticed Sinclair's headgear, 'Canny cap that, like!'

Sinclair wasn't sure what he had just heard, - he wasn't even sure in which language he had been addressed - but he dutifully followed the opposing captain. A few choice words from the H... captain sent half a dozen youths scurrying from the field, and together, the captains went to the middle to perform the pre-match ritual of the coin toss.

After winning, the toss, and making a show of studying the pitch Harvey St Jean Sinclair announced, 'We'll bowl, I think; there's a few green spots which my quickies should be able to exploit.'

There wasn't and they didn't. The home side amassed 172 for 4 in their twenty overs. The head teacher was not amused: he should have realised that his team of conscripts were not taking the challenge seriously when, insisting that the ball be passed to him for the ritualistic shining, he discovered that it had been smeared in green phlegm. The culprit was never uncovered. His frustration turned to anger when it became apparent that a variety of vile noises and smells emanating from the cordon of slip fielders had been employed to try and unsettle the opposition batsmen.

Arguments among the outfielders were frequent. They performed as if they would rather be anywhere but here. And not without good reason, for as well as having to suffer abuse from the crowd, they were always mindful of the posse of assorted whippets and bull terriers which seemed to strain at their lease, every time a visiting fielder ventured to field a ball near the boundary edge!

As The Townies prepared for their innings, the head teacher did his best to encourage and cajole his troops. Almost to a man, they looked knackered: they had been obliged to fetch and carry the ball from every inch of the ground.

Inevitably, Harvey St Jean Sinclair opened the batting for his school. As he had explained in his team talk, he would be the rock on which the quest for victory would be built. He thought his pep-talk would inspire his team to victory against all the odds. His 'men' did not seem to agree; in fact they did not seem to be listening, as, to a man, they were focusing on the H... opening bowler marking out his run-up, and coming back almost to the pavilion.

The innings couldn't have started more badly: the opening bowler's first ball, pitched in his half of the wicket, and fizzed and whizzed past Harvey St Jean Sinclair's cap. The blood drained from his face. The second ball was fuller and straighter, and smashed into the captain's bat, almost knocking it from his hands. 'Run,' he shrieked, and set off for the safety of the non-striker's end. His fellow opening batsman didn't stand a chance, and he was run out by the proverbial mile. Not that he was bothered one little bit. A smile was just visible on the young teacher's lips.

'You should have been backing up,' his captain admonished his fellow opener, with a rueful shake of his head.

'My arse,' the young teacher muttered to himself, clearly thankful that he was out of the firing line.

The school team were in further trouble when batsmen 3, 4 and 5 succumbed without troubling the scorers, grateful to have survived with their bodies intact.

With the score at 7 for 4 the opposing captain removed the fearsome pace bowler from the attack. St Jean Sinclair walked down the wicket to consult with the new batsman; 'Now's the time to make them pay; we'll get them in singles if we have to. Just remember to run the first run quickly, and put pressure on the fielders.'

The new batsman nodded his understanding. He was in fact, not a bad cricketer; he was new to the school, and saw this as his opportunity to impress his colleagues, and especially his head teacher. A good innings couldn't harm his future prospects for promotion.

The head teacher nodded his appreciation as young Gary went through the batting rituals: he asked for 'two legs', scraped his mark with the toe of his boot, looked around at the field placing, adjusted his box, sneaked another look at the fielders (in case one had cunningly moved), and settled down to face his first delivery. The head teacher was very impressed.

Gary snicked the first ball down to third man. He set off immediately, head down, remembering to 'run the first run hard.' On reaching the bowler's end, Gary relaxed: he had avoided the dreaded 'golden duck.' Looking up, Gary noticed that the fielder at third man had slipped, and fallen over.

Realising that he could double his tally, and more importantly, reclaim the strike, he raced back down the wicket. Harvey St Jean Sinclair was nonplussed, but acknowledging that it was Gary's call, he complied with the yelled command to run.

The wicket keeper could not believe his eyes. With sadistic relish, he smashed down the stumps, running Gary out even before he was halfway down the wicket. The fielder had fallen and slipped, *after* he had thrown the ball!

Laughter could be heard all round the ground as fielders and spectators alike revelled in Gary's discomfort against a chorus of braying donkey noises, as he made his way back down the wicket, past his head teacher to the dressing room.

Thanks to the generosity of the opposing captain who removed the most lethal front line bowlers from the attack, Harvey St Jean Sinclair managed to keep his wicket intact. His score even reached double figures, all singles. Not that the batsmen at the other end were bothered; they were quite happy to watch the Head prove himself to be a prize prat. He would move away from his wicket whenever jeers and crude remarks from the spectators reached him.

'Get on with it, you ponce! It's not a fucking test match!' bellowed one supporter. The next ball rapped Harvey St Jean Sinclair on the pads.

'Owzat' the bowler appealed, with no enthusiasm, as the ball was clearly missing. It wouldn't even have hit another set of stumps. The umpire had clearly had enough, or had been rendered comatose by the inactivity, and his he raised his finger.

Harvey St Jean Sinclair stood in disbelief. But mindful of his position as captain, and above all, head teacher, he gave an almost imperceptible shake of the head, and walked from the wicket.

Opposition fielders sniggered like naughty schoolboys, but were keen to see the mismatch brought to a close. As the Head walked off, the fielder at mid-off announced, 'Bad luck.'

'Thank you.' Sinclair replied.

'No; for us, we were trying to keep you in!' and he moved off to join his team mates in their ridicule of the departing batsman.

The number nine batsman passed his captain, head down, not wanting to have to sympathise.

Back in the dressing room, the Head accepted the sympathy of the other players.

'Look,' the Head said, 'we can still win this.' As heads turned away, he added, 'If anyone doesn't agree with me...' He left his veiled threat unfinished, but he added to nobody in particular, 'Maybe that's why I'm a head teacher, and you're not.'

The dressing room went quiet, and when another wicket fell, the batsman caught at short leg, from a ball which smashed into his wrist, the Head tried once more to rally his troops. 'Don't panic,' he advocated, to be immediately mimicked by a member of his staff, clearly a fan of Dad's Army,

'Don't panic, Captain...'

'As I was saying...' the Head resumed, after the sniggers had died down, only for him to be interrupted again by another voice, this time in a mock, exaggerated Scottish accent,

'We're doomed...' This time the sniggers became guffaws, and the Head decided to leave the dressing room, and watch the rest of the innings from the veranda.

Bob the caretaker was sitting with his pads on, waiting his turn to go in to bat. He didn't have long to wait, as a loud appeal was followed by clapping as the umpire upheld the home bowler's appeal. He flicked his cigarette away, put on his batting gloves, and prepared to venture forth.

Before he descended the pavilion steps, Bob was stopped by the head teacher.

'Bob, I've had an idea: it's getting a bit murky, so I want you to appeal against the light, and we'll have another go at them when we've got a stronger side out.'

Bob nodded his comprehension. 'But Bob,' the Head added, 'I want you to be subtle. Have a look at it, and then appeal.'

Bob nodded again. He descended the steps, and waddled his way to the middle. He was hardly what you would call an athlete, and players and spectators alike sniggered as he approached the crease.

It was hard to believe that this un-athletic figure was, in fact, not a bad cricketer, or at least he had been before age, alcohol and dietary abuse had taken their toll. The Head had been more than a little annoyed when he'd gone to pick up the caretaker at his bungalow after school had finished. He'd had to wait as Bob finished his tea, a huge portion of chicken masala. He was unimpressed that Bob was not taking things seriously, and told him so.

'But I am, sir,' Bob responded, 'I only had one naan bread instead of three.' As the Head's face registered incomprehension, Bob added, 'And I didn't have any poppadoms.

And I only had half of lager.' Harvey St Jean Sinclair had said nothing; he decided to concentrate on his driving.

Bob arrived at the crease with the words of his captain in his ears. He didn't bother to take a guard, and as instructed by his captain, he left the first two deliveries. The third ball was pitched up to him, and Bob couldn't resist: his mantra had always been 'If the ball is up to you, twat it!' And twat it he did! The ball sailed into the nearby cemetery. The next ball was bludgeoned straighter and further, over the clubhouse, before landing in the street.

Then, remembering his captain's instructions, Bob turned to the umpire and said, 'Can I appeal against the light?'

The umpire could not believe his ears.

'But you've just put two out of the ground.'

'I know, but if I'd been able to see, I'd have put them out of the fucking village.'

Bob's efforts were in vain: the H... bowlers mopped up the tail condemning the 'posh townies' to a humiliating thrashing.

The post-match refreshments were held in the village working men's club, a legacy of the region's coal mining industry, and still a bastion of socialism. Harvey St John Sinclair tried to put a brave face on the humiliating debacle, but in the Big Club, he was clearly a fish out of water as he stood at the bar sipping his Amaretto and ice (complete with cocktail cherry!), his lemon coloured cashmere jumper draped round his shoulders. And he had felt compelled to leave early after again bringing ridicule on himself. When served his pie and mushy peas, he had proclaimed, 'Oh I do like a spot of guacamole.'

'Yeah, right!' a rough voice announced, heavy with sarcasm, 'We've brought in a chef from the Michelin star restaurant round the corner!' The Big Club had resounded with mocking laughter!

In the car during the return journey, Bob felt obliged to apologise to his captain. 'Forget it Bob; you did us all a favour. At least we don't have to come back to this shithole.'

Startled by the vehemence of his reply, the Head glanced uncomfortably at Bob. Then, embarrassed by his coarse outburst in front of his caretaker, and his rare lack of composure, Harvey St Jean Sinclair gripped the steering wheel, and concentrated on the road back to town.

Bob smiled to himself. 'That's more like it. Join the club, and welcome to the north-east.' Nevertheless, he might just start taking bets on how long this southern softie would survive in the grim north.

THE NOBLEST PROFESSION OF ALL?

'God! I bloody hate Monday mornings!' muttered Mark (Albi) Senior as he rummaged through the mangled metal locker for the dozen misshapen plastic rugby balls, still caked in mud since they were last used goodness knows when! 'Now where the hell is that pump?'

He started to pump up the balls, unable to put the shitty weekend out of his mind: a skinful of beer, followed by a double portion of fish'n'chips in a greasy chippie in downtown Birkenhead had started the damage. Then, their departure had been delayed, because the police had been called after punches had been thrown; why, he asked himself, had their stupid captain caused the trouble? Why could he not have asked for fish or jumbo sausage and chips like everyone else? Why had he asked for nigger's dick and chips? He hadn't known the owner was West Indian, but even so…

Then the ordeal of a four hour journey on the team bus back over the Pennines, with the stink of stale beer, tobacco and unlit farts, had just about finished him off. Sleep was virtually impossible, of course; pee-stops every half hour or so, followed by the obligatory scuffles on the back seats, had seen to that. The driver seemed to have had a few beers as well, and had mounted the pavement more than once.

Albi had just nodded off, as the bus came into town. He was soon woken by raucous shouts from every section of the bus. Somebody close to him bellowed 'Next corner, driver!', and a seventeen stone forward clawed and scrambled over the seat near him.

Eventually, it was his turn to get off; wearing only his thin club blazer, and carrying his scruffy holdall, he trudged the half mile to his home. '4:30 am! Jesus!'

Normally, he would have recovered on Sunday, but he'd been woken by the phone at 9:00 am. It was the captain of the Sunday League football team asking, no, demanding, that he turn out to play, so that the team would not forfeit the cup match for not fielding a full side. What was worse, they had stuck him in goal.

A 7-2 defeat on a filthy freezing pitch was bad enough, but he had actually got himself sent off, for punching the opposition centre forward who had tried to head-butt him as they went up for the ball together. He might even have slept on Sunday afternoon, but he'd had to go to his in-laws for Sunday lunch. He couldn't stand the bickering between his mother- and father-in-law. This time, an argument had started from nowhere, about the skin on the rice pudding! To put the cap on a lousy weekend, he'd had to spend three hours that evening writing reports for his poxy Year 10 classes. If only he'd been able to write what he really thought of these revolting little cretins! But no; the Deputy Head had insisted that the reports be positive, to encourage them to greater things. Who did he think he was kidding?

Albi couldn't even remember driving to school. A couple of Benson & Hedges and three cups of black coffee seemed to have had no effect. He knew he should quit smoking; his intake of booze and ciggies was taking its toll on both his health and his wallet! And maybe as a PE teacher, he should set an example to his pupils; but he knew that many of them smoked - and drank - more than he did. How could they afford it?

He knew the answer without ever having to ask them; there was a healthy black market on the estate around the school and a number of his pupils regularly went AWOL as they accompanied parents and uncles on the booze-and-fags runs to the channel ports. Some of the cheeky little buggers even tried to sell him fags and beer!

Albi's first job was to check the 'sick notes.' This didn't usually take long as he knew all the malingerers, and most made it easy for him by presenting the sick note on paper torn from an exercise book. 'Forgery!'

he announced to the first youth. 'Get changed quickly.' He repeated the routine half a dozen times.

Albi then had to make sure the class left the changing room; the lazy sods knew all manner of tricks to avoid their weekly exercise and pain - hiding in the showers and in the gym among the equipment, under gymnastic mats (with their mates sitting on them!), and even, on one occasion, inside the vaulting horse. He smiled at the memory, admiring their ingenuity, but he too had watched the film on television depicting a breakout by prisoners of war from Stalag Luft III.

Albi's mind only started to focus when he left the sports hall. He zipped up his anorak, and turned up the collar, before venturing forth.

Struggling to keep hold of the rugby balls, as the biting north-easterly wind and sleet whipped across the exposed school playing field, he turned to enter the school field. As usual, that dozy little twat Jenkins was waiting for him, fussing like the daft little sod that he was. 'Is it rugby today, sir?' he asked.

'Naw, power boat racing!' Albi snapped. 'God! There must be more to life than this!'

CPSIA information can be obtained at www.ICGtesting.com
Printed in the USA
LVOW04s2350131014

408538LV00025B/866/P